CW00506786

Gallery Books
Editor Peter Fallon

LIFE ON EARTH

Derek Mahon

LIFE ON EARTH

Gallery Books

Life on Earth
is first published
simultaneously in paperback
and in a clothbound edition
on 9 October 2008.

The Gallery Press
Loughcrew
Oldcastle
County Meath
Ireland

www.gallerypress.com

ISBN 978 1 85235 461 9 *paperback*
978 1 85235 462 6 *clothbound*

A CIP catalogue record for this book
is available from the British Library.

Contents

Ariadne on Naxos 11
Biographia Literaria 13
Trigorin 15
Brian Moore's Belfast 17
Quaderno 19
Insomnia 22
Somewhere the Wave 24
Tara Boulevard 25
Goa 26
Circe and Sirens 27
The Lady from the Sea 29
Art Notes
   1 A Lighthouse in Maine 31
   2 The Realm of Light 32
   3 Studio in Antibes 33
   4 Cushendun in Winter 34
   5 Birds 35
   6 Rain 36
   7 Wave Shadow 37
   8 Savannah Dock 38
   9 Triptych 39
The Clifden Road 40
Research 41
A Country Road 42
Homage to Gaia
   1 Its Radiant Energies 44
   2 Homage to Gaia 46
   3 Wind and Wave 47
   4 Sand and Stars 49
   5 At Ursula's 50
   6 London Rain 52
   7 Ode to Björk 54
   8 Dirigibles 56
   9 Indian Garden 58
Turtle Beach 59
Homage to Goa 60

for Jane and Maisie

Ariadne on Naxos

(Ovid, *Heroides* X)

Above the cold beach and the pounding waves,
Theseus, your wretched Ariadne grieves.
(I write this in our hut behind the strand
with hidden birds chirping along the coast.)
You were worse than a beast, at least a beast
would have some pity for its own kind.
Abruptly waking, knowing you weren't here,
I scrambled up, struck by a sudden fear,
and ran down in time to see the sun rise
as your sail opened in the morning breeze.
Distraught and furious, my clothes undone,
I stood there shrieking like a madwoman
or some lost Maenad, while the waves rose
to thigh and hip; and there my heart froze
watching you go, me with my failing strength
who rescued you from the dark labyrinth.
There's no one here, no one to help me leave
this barren place, and even if there were
where would I go? I can't go home alive,
I who betrayed Crete to the foreigner.
Without my guidance and the spool of thread
I gave you in the maze, you would be dead.
'As long as we both live' was what you said.
We're both alive, I think, but not together
and now I know what the abandoned suffer.
Besides, I'm frightened that at any time
wolves may appear and tear me limb from limb
— or even men, who frighten me now too:
I've no faith left in people I don't know.
I wish I'd never saved your life back there.
Of course you overcame the Minotaur:
you'd no need of a shield to protect you,
not even those long horns could penetrate

a heart harder than flint, sharper than slate.
Am I to die here? Will my body lie
exposed to buzzards watching from the sky
or will some kind god take pity on me?
When you get home, famous, and at the dock
tell them the story of the Cretan cave
include the love your Ariadne gave
before you left her here on this bare rock.

Biographia Literaria

(Samuel Taylor Coleridge, 1772-1834)

A spoilt child shivers at the river's edge —
night-hiding yes but anxious to be found,
a troubled soul torn between fear and rage.
Sun, moon and star on the sky-blue clock face
in the south transept of St. Mary's mind
the autumn dark, and shadows have changed place
obscurely, each tick an 'articulate sound',
as he dozes off under a rustic bridge.

When he wakes at dawn to a slow-waning moon,
frozen and scared, curled up like the unborn,
the sun blinking behind an owl-eyed barn,
frost in the fields and winter coming on,
a frigate flutters on a glittering sea.
A great cold has gripped the heart already
with signs of witchery in an ivy tree:
now nothing will ever be the same again.

Genie, taper and paper, long solitary cliff walks,
cloud thoughts unfolding over the Quantocks
sheer to shore beneath high, feathery springs.
The cottage shines its light above the rocks,
the world's oceans tear in from the west
and an Aeolian harp the size of a snuff-box
sings in a casement where its tingling strings
record the faintest whisper, the loudest blast.

Receptive, tense, adrift in a breezy trance,
the frame is seized as if in a nightmare
by some quotation, fugue, some fugitive air,
some distant echo of the primal scream.
Silence, dead calm, no worldly circumstance;
the words form figures and begin to dance —

and then the miracle, the pleasure dome,
the caves of ice, the vibrant dulcimer.

Stowey to Göttingen, philosophy in a mist,
wide-eyed sublimities of ghost and *Geist*,
wild wind-and-rain effects of Greta Hall,
the rattling windows and the icy lake,
babbling excursions and the perpetual
white roaring rose of a close waterfall;
finally Highgate Grove and table talk,
a 'destined harbour' for the afflicted soul.

Asra and Christabel in confused opium dreams,
heartbroken whimpers and nocturnal screams
grow ever fainter as he becomes 'a sage
escaped from the inanity', aghast
at furious London and its rising smoke,
the sinister finance of a dark new age.
Dunn's pharmacy is only a short walk;
his grown-up daughter visits him there at last.

Trigorin

(Chekhov, *The Seagull,* Act 4)

The towns where the train pauses manufacture
chimneys and fences, boredom, mud and birches.
A cool breeze flaps decrepit architecture
and blows a white blaze on the country roads,
vegetable gardens, grimy local churches.
Folk-tale heroines nap in the autumn woods;
at Tver', only a hundred versts from Moscow,
a wandering gull foreshadows the first snow.

The clouds are grand pianos; he makes a note.
Gogolian porters blink in smoky shadows,
a scent of heliotrope and a buzz of flies.
Girl in a blouse, man in a linen suit;
the wind goes running in remembered meadows
under the vast light of these northern skies:
'Out here I feel a quickening of the senses
far from reviewers and hostile audiences.'

Nina, he's come this time for a last look
at the great forest and your native lake,
the clear freshwater ripples you deserted
to join the theatre for his sake and yours.
He let you down of course, and himself too:
his work fell off when he lost sight of you.
Your soul migrated from his icy art;
a stuffed gull listens from a chest of drawers.

Watch out, he's working on a new novel,
his best yet; when it sees the light of day
critics, as usual, will find it slight,
adroitly done though not a patch on Tolstoy.
(So too the friends gathered around his grave:
'Oh, a great gift, if not quite Turgenev . . .')

A dead seagull, what a terrific story;
amazing if you too were there tonight —

and there you are now, tapping the windowpane
like a tense revenant or a familiar ghost.
Waves on the water, wind loud in the wood
with a raw October evening drawing in,
but nobody loves each other as they should.
All come and go, to the hotel, the train,
the gun room and the veranda; all begin
to die, it will be twenty years at most.

Brian Moore's Belfast

(for Gerald Dawe)

The last trams were still running in those days.
People wore hats and gloves as long before;
raw fissures lingered where incendiaries
demolished Clifton St. in April of '41:
the big band era, dances and commotion,
but the war ended and rain swept once more
parks and playgrounds, chapel and horse trough
'to die in the faraway mists over Belfast Lough'.

Do this, do that, road closed, no entry, stop! —
a world of signs and yet the real thing too:
even now I catch a whiff of brack and bap,
the soap and ciggies of the *disparus*.
Buns from Stewart's, gobstoppers from Graham's,
our crowd intent on our traditional games,
sectarian puzzlement, a swinging rope,
freezing winters, pristine bicycle frames;

school windows under the Cave Hill, childish faces,
uncles and aunties, pipes and lipstick traces,
epiphanies in sheds and woody places:
how can we not love the first life we knew?
'We can dream only what we know,' he said.
I know the whole length of the Antrim Road
and often think of Salisbury Avenue;
mysterious Hazelwood, I still dream of you.

On Riverside Drive and a California dream beach
such things revisited him, just out of reach,
just as he left them after Naples, Warsaw,
frozen for ever in the austere post-war
where frequent silence keeps its own integrity
and smoky ghosts of the exhausted city

rustle with phantom life whose time is up.
They queue in Campbell's crowded coffee shop

or wait for a bus at Robb's. I can make out
a clutch of gantries, a white sepulchre
grimly vigilant on its tiny acre,
skirts and shirts mid-20th-century style
in dimly lit arcades, carpets of wet
grain at the quayside where a night boat
churns up the dark and a rapturous old girl
sings 'Now is the Hour' with her eternal smile.

Quaderno

I AN ICE-CREAM AT CAPRONI'S

— Bangor, 1939

She sits there tinkering with an ice-cream
of many colours, lost in a private dream;
she wears a hat, gloves and a frilly blouse
and shivers slightly in a summer breeze:
if only time could stop like this before
life choices, childbirth and the coming war.

2 BEYOND THE ALPS

He slopes off into the snow without his skis.
Gudrun sees him vanish: what can she do
as he goes ghost-like under lowering skies?
Blind hut, dim crucifix, while far below
the inn lights and the old imperial road
point to the happier lives they might have led.

3 CASA SUL MARE

A sheet of morning mist and a light breeze
lull self-effacing waves and cavities.
No sparkling breakers and no flying foam;
but it still waits for you, that little room
in this remembering house, your hands and eyes
plumping the pillows, making yourself at home.

4 DIOGENES ON THE SHORE

I want no strangers standing in my light,
their hearts at peace, and I deplore the sight

of tedious tourists with their cine-cameras
spoiling our quiet vistas and panoramas.
We spend our days conversing with chimeras
and take a torch when we go out at night.

5 GERONIMO

'Geronimo!', I thought, when an Etruscan
appeared in a drowsy garage at Cerveteri.
He had the earthy look of primitive man,
carried himself like a spry veteran
of tribal conflict, disinherited yet
blithe, and took off in an ancient Fiat.

6 PASOLINI

Cruising for wild *ragazzi* out of season,
he sat late at Giordano's and drove down
in his Alfa Romeo to the seaplane basin
where, knifed and mangled in the sand and ash,
a wreck but recognizable, he lives on
as a bronze bird-shape shining amid the trash.

7 I PENSIEROSI

We too spent time in the high lonely tower,
bricks and bridges fading from rose to grey,
the anglepoise tilted at midnight hour
with other lamps aglow in Fiesole,
a silent fountain and an ivy hedge
reflecting the grave thoughts of middle age.

8 PAOLO AND LIGHEA

A young man slept with a mermaid one fine night
in the blue depths of an Ischian sea-cave
where 'she ate nothing that was not alive',
and nothing since has ever been quite right.
He lives alone now, unlike you and me,
his briny heart nostalgic for the sea.

9 BEATRICE HASTINGS

'I retain only memories and pictures,
stirring and palpable, perhaps overdone
in homage to your most endearing features;
also your verses, dance routines and one
or two love phrases, intimate and funny,
murmured to your admirer, Modigliani.'

10 '. . . DOVE PER SOLE . . .'
— *Dino Campana*

I loved you in a city where the solitary
step rings in an empty thoroughfare
eirenic dusk relieves with a rain shower
and the incorrigible heart once more
turns to an ambiguous spring in violet
distances beyond the washed-out sky.

Insomnia

Scratch of a match
fierce in the dark. The alarm clock,
night-vigilant, reads twenty minutes to four;
wide awake, as so often at this dead hour,
I gaze down at the lighted dock,
trawler and crated catch,
as if on watch.

The bright insects
of helicopters drop to the decks
of gas rigs ten miles out in the heavy waves,
their roaring rotors far from our quiet leaves,
before midnight, and the ship that shone
at dusk on the horizon
has long since gone.

Nothing stirs
in garden or silent house,
no night owl flies or none that we can hear;
not even the mild, traditional field-mouse
runs nibbling, as you'd expect, under the stairs.
Boats knock and click at the pier,
shrimps worship the stars.

The whole coast
is soporific as if lost
to echoes of a distant past —
the empty beach house with no obvious owner,
the old hotel like a wrecked ocean liner
washed up one stormy night
and left to rot.

That woman from
the Seaview, a 'blow-in'
of some kind from a foreign shore,

seems out of her element and far from home,
the once perhaps humorous eyes grown vague out here.
What is she? A Lithuanian, or a Finn?
We've met before

beside some flat
road bridge or bleak strand road,
two men in black at the corner staring hard,
far off in the stricken distance perhaps a shipyard,
chimneys, power plants, gasometers,
oil refineries, Gothic spires
and things like that —

where a cloud climbs
and swirls, yellow and red
streaking the estuary, and a soul screams
for sunken origins, for the obscure sea bed
and glowing depths, the alternative mud haven
we left behind. Once more we live in
interesting times.

Somewhere the Wave

Once more the window and a furious fly
shifting position, niftier on the pane
than the slow liner or the tiny plane.
Dazzled by the sun, dazed by the rain,
today this frantic speck against the sky,
so desperate to get out in the open air
and cruise among the roses, starts to know
not all transparency is come and go.

But the window opens like an opened door
so the wild fly escapes to the airstream,
the raw crescendo of the crashing shore
and 'a radical astonishment at existence' —
a voice, not quite a voice, in the sea distance
listening to its own thin cetaceous whistle,
sea music gasp and sigh, slow wash and rustle.
Somewhere the wave is forming which in time . . .

Tara Boulevard

Amazed by the shining towers were she alive,
she wouldn't know the downtown skyline now
— Coke, Delta Airlines, CNN, King Drive —
but ten miles south, in many a back yard,
it's going to be another day tomorrow
on an imaginary plantation where
the Ibo sat once to their hominy grits;
in Jonesboro, 'O'Hara Gas and Body Parts'
light up at dusk on Tara Boulevard,
red neon scribbling to the thundery air.

Goa

Even now I think of you with a kind of awe.
Do you laze this evening on an 'azure' shore,
you whom I last saw twenty years ago,
or contemplate from a beach house in Goa
the Indian Ocean breaking on the coast
where my love, gratitude and grief lie waste?
If only we'd fought off the final row;
but, poets both, we saw the drama through.
Decades divide us from the life we lost
and only in spirit can I be with you now.

Circe and Sirens

Homer was right to break the story up —
flash back, fast forward to another beach,
another island. As the sun rose and shone
they headed inland and found Circe's place
in its dim glade, a pavilion of white stone,
a ribbon of woodsmoke rising from the thatch
where wolves and lions, dozy from sedatives,
lived out their nodding, soporific lives;
the men, recovered from her magic cup,
relaxed and sprawled at ease about the house.

He took the prophylactic. 'Sail,' she said,
'over the water to the Cimmerian coast,
those dark people shrouded in fog and mist.
Beside a grim, fast-flowing river bed
there is a grove where rustling willows grow;
dig a trench there out of the leafy mud
and you will see a multitude of the dead,
their curious shadows whispering to and fro,
come up to look at you. Amid that host
speak to your mother and Tiresias' ghost.'

Among the wives and daughters of the great
— Jocasta, Ariadne, Phaedra — he came upon
his mother Anticleia who whispered 'Son,
this is no place for you, why are you here
with these lost spirits? What capricious fate
brings you among us before your time is due?'
Tiresias appeared. 'You will be late
in getting home,' said he, 'in a bad state,
with a strange ship, all your companions gone;
yet you will die contented and ashore.'

And there he recognized young Elpenor,
a foolish drunken fellow who'd slept off
a party on the tiles and with the dawn,
woken up by the others' rush and din,
stumbled and fell headlong from Circe's roof.
'Remember me,' he cried. 'Burn my remains,
bury my ashes on the grey sea-shore
and for a gravestone plant the shapely oar
I pulled when I was alive among my friends.'
The thing was done and they set off once more.

The Sirens sang: 'Odysseus, slow down! —
Sailors who hear us from their painted ships
never forget the sweet sound of our voices,
the enchanted music issuing from our lips';
but, agitated and wild-eyed, he sailed on
to thundering cave and overhanging cliff,
loud breakers, wandering rocks and sucking surf.
Sheet lightning tore the timbers from their places
and corpses bobbed like seagulls on the sea;
but, clinging to a spar, he floated free.

'. . . if you survive,' Tiresias warned, 'the few
remaining dangers you have yet to face
and the temptations being prepared for you.'
Dangers he had expected, not another
island, its dune songs and erotic weather
where he might stop indefinitely moreover
and his restorative visit last for years.
He might retire, sea music in his ears,
this micro-climate his last resting place,
and spend his old age in sublime disgrace.

The Lady from the Sea

(after Ibsen)

She Born in a lighthouse, I still find it hard
as wife to a doctor ten miles from the coast.
My home is a pleasant one but I get bored;
the mountains bother me. Now, like a ghost,
you show up here, severe and adamant.
What are you anyhow? What do you want?

He I am a simple man upon the land,
I am a seal upon the open sea.
Your eyes are of the depths. Give me your hand,
give me your heart and come away with me
to the Spice Islands, the South Seas; anywhere.
Only the force of habit keeps you here.

She Even up here, enclosed, I sniff the brine,
the open sea out there beyond the beach;
my thoughts are waves, my dreams are estuarine
and deeper than an anchor chain could reach.
I knew you'd come, like some demonic fate
glimpsed at a window or a garden gate.

He How can you live here with no real horizon,
someone like you, a mermaid and a Muse,
a figment of your own imagination,
the years elapsing like a tedious cruise?
Your settled life is like this summer glow;
dark clouds foreshadow the approaching snow.

She Sometimes, emerging from my daily swim
or gazing from the dock these quiet nights,
I know my siren soul; and in a dream
I stare astonished at the harbour lights,

hugging my knees and sitting up alone
as ships glide darkly past with a low moan.

He If our mad race had never left the sea,
had we remained content with mud and rock,
we might have saved ourselves great misery;
though even this evening we might still go back.
Think of the crashing breakers, the dim haze
of a salt sun rising on watery days.

She My wild spirit unbroken, should I return
to the tide, choosing at last my other life,
reverting to blue water and sea-brine,
or do I continue as a faithful wife?
If faithful is the word for one who clings
to the lost pre-existence of previous things.

He Do you remember the great vow you made
to the one man you chose from other men?
The years have come between, with nothing said,
and now the stranger has appeared again
to claim your former love and make it new.
You ask me what I am; but what are you?

She I am a troubled woman on the land,
I am a seal upon the open sea,
but it's too late to give my heart and hand
to someone who remains a mystery.
Siren or not, this is my proper place;
go to your ship and leave me here in peace.

Art Notes

I A LIGHTHOUSE IN MAINE

— Edward Hopper

It might be anywhere, that ivory tower
reached by a country road. Granite and sky,
it faces every which way with an air
of squat omniscience, intensely mild,
a polished Buddha figure warm and dry
beyond vegetation; and the sunny glare
striking its shingled houses is no more
celestial than the hot haze of the world.

Built to shed light but also hoarding light,
it sits there dozing in the afternoon
above the ocean like a ghostly moon
patiently waiting to illuminate.
You make a left beyond the town, a right,
you turn a corner and there, ivory-white,
it shines in modest glory above a bay.
Out you get and walk the rest of the way.

2 THE REALM OF LIGHT

— *René Magritte*

The picture in the picture window shows
a poplar, is it, a house calm and clear
at dawn or dusk, a lamp post's yellow light
abuzz on shutters and a shivering pond.
Poplar and roof aspire though, point beyond
the upstairs reading lamp to another sphere
where, behind deckled leaves, pacific rows
of cloud file slowly past, serenely white.

It must be dusk, with the light almost gone,
but view this picture with extreme distrust
since what you see is the *trompe-l'oeil* of dream.
It *might* be dusk, with the house almost dead;
or is there somebody getting out of bed,
the exhausted street light anxious for a rest,
birds waking in the trees, the clouds astream
in an invisible breeze? It must be dawn.

3 STUDIO IN ANTIBES

— Nicolas de Staël

'Waiting on chance to get the pictures out
otherwise locked in the chromatic brain,
I've worked the nerves into a curious state,
talk only to my models and sleep alone.
Je sais que ma solitude est inhumaine.
Here I renounce abstraction, turning again
to the world of objects, to the stoical souls
of candlesticks and jugs, bottles and bowls.

'After the blue nudes the attentive studio
fills up again with coffee, bread and fruit,
with sun and sky, white gulls in sudden flight
when I open the window on a misty night,
rocks and a lighthouse, fishing boats in port;
but paint can't give me what I need to know.
A yellow concert starts up in my head,
soon growing in volume as it turns to red.'

4 CUSHENDUN IN WINTER

— Maurice Wilks

North light on the snowlight on a little bridge
where once we loitered during a previous age
in the quiet dusk of one more summer day
as the sun went down behind the Antrim hills
and Scotland dimly shone across the water.
Girls watched the boys go by, the boys the girls,
the Lavery sisters and the postman's daughter;
later we'd flirt with them at Lynn's Café.

Wilks never bothered with 'the picture plane',
with 'colour values' and the fancy words —
as for aesthetics, that was for the birds.
They slept in a yellow trailer at Shane's Cairn
where, every morning, he would paint the world:
hedges, fields, the sunlight on the river,
the forest and the dunes, a still unspoiled
paradise we thought would last for ever.

5 BIRDS

— Georges Braque

(after Saint-John Perse)

The swift plunge of the artist, raptor and rapt,
seizes them in a flash and flings them down
on the lithographic plate, there to be shaped
for the sky-page, printed though never trapped;
their brows those of dolphins or the newborn,
gathered like ghosts, unmindful of their own
shadows, they fly to their remote wing songs
leaving us silent in the bronze of gongs.

Day being too short for them, they cruise at night.
Stripped for action, slick as spacecraft, driven
by two strokes to the spectral limits of flight,
they move like language to a cosmic rhythm,
like wind-blown paper, leaves or tongues of flame.
Blurring the moon, they glide down tracts of time;
abstracted from the facts and lost to sight,
they save for us something of the creative dream.

6 RAIN

— *Howard Hodgkin*

Some kind of board and an old frame will do
for his strong hues and open brush strokes.
This sodden emerald, this windswept blue
roaring into the back yard, oil on wood,
are representational though not wholly so
being largely 'about paint' and the residue
of primitive alchemy in the dreamworks:
he'd make gold in a piss-pot if he could.

Bombay is a pretext for hot yellow and brown
where a tandoori sun has just gone down;
the lovers, a frank swirl of head-to-head
organic shapes, are ginger on gland-red,
two spicy colours making violent love;
and the long breakers in a briny cove
streaming exultantly on the bread board
are black and blue come quick into their own.

7 WAVE SHADOW

— Vivienne Roche

Of glass and bronze, it gasps and faintly heaves,
cascading down like rain or up like leaves
in a light breeze, and rippling ridges hear
a chattering atrium or an echoing pool
with its clinical, brain-rinsing atmosphere.
You could float here for ever, blue and cool,
waves sloshing round the details that refer
sidelong to Hokusai, to Neolithic caves

and the blue dolphins in Ariadne's bedroom
chuckling and diving up there even now.
Wave theory liberates the ebb and flow:
where will the drip drop or the foam form,
what dim considerations move the cloud?
What more in heaven and in the sea below?
A gleaming boardwalk bridges the divide
from raw experience to the other side.

8 SAVANNAH DOCK

— Anthony Palliser

(*for Diane*)

There you are, coming from your wooden wharf
as if in a photograph or a home movie.
Perhaps you've been for a swim, a lazy sail
on the great river, 'wider than a mile',
or out to sea to where the Gullah live
in their sea islands and the heavy surf,
a thundering ocean, throws up African stuff.
The sun is shining and you look lovely.

The green light at the end of Daisy's dock
and Gatsby's crazy parties at Great Neck
are worlds away from your own natural space
where an unmeretricious real moon shines
and stars are mild above the Georgia pines.
May life be gentle in your scented air
and the art flourish that you nourish there
in peace and quiet, far from the marketplace.

9 TRIPTYCH

(*for Anne Madden*)

Pompeiian door frames, crimson and ultramarine
air boxes choking with black smoke and ash
blow clear to sea-light like a tambourine.
The sun's forge, a gold continuous crash,
roars and flickers with perpetual flames;
winged figures circulate in the airstreams
and an ill-fated one, having flown too high,
drops into legend through a whirling sky.

Hang-gliding in the sun like Saint-Exupéry
the hawk or lapwing, a brave girl or boy,
dives to the gravitational field of the sea,
one tiny lifeboat like an abandoned toy
or its own shadow: picture the climax though,
the wild euphoria when for a minute or so,
deaf to the crackling kite tackle of gravity,
it flaps there treading air in a hot glow.

Space-time is a spun network where it falls
to a dash of paint and graphite, inks and oils,
dense atmospherics, bright transparencies.
Night comes with cloudy hands, the windy skies
are 'filled with graves', but a night garden fills
with moonlit palms, cicadas, murmuring souls;
blue-white and luminous in a partial dark,
your stairs lead up to the calm house of work.

The Clifden Road

(after Michel Houellebecq)

West of Clifden on a cliff
where sky changes into sea
and sea to memory as if
at the edge of a new world

on the long hills of Clifden
the green hills of Clifden
I will lay down my grief.

To accept death it must be
that death changes into light
that light changes into sea
and sea into memory.

The far west of human life
lies on the Clifden road
the long Clifden road
where man lays down his grief
between the waves and the light.

Research

An actual conch
like a human head on its side,
washed up and left here by the ebb tide,
a magical sculpture, perfectly arbitrary,
lies as if dropped from orbit.
Oh, they will launch

research to find
ice in the Sea of Rains,
a first dubious twitch of mud and plants,
signs of life on the other planets,
whispers of inchoate mind
and flickering brains.

Meanwhile on Earth
we've mud, plants, pleasure, pain
and even real lives to be getting on with;
seasons for this and that, the works and days
of many mice and men
as Hesiod says.

Best to ignore
'the great ocean of truth',
the undiscovered seas of outer space,
and research this real unconscious conch on the shore
with its polished, archaic face
and its air of myth.

A Country Road

Above rising crops
the sun peeps like an eclipse
in a snow of hawthorn, and a breeze sings
its simple pleasure in the nature of things,
a tinkling ditch and a long field
where tractors growled.

Second by second
cloud swirls on the globe as though
political; lilacs listen to the wind,
watching birds circle in the yellow glow
of a spring day, in a sea stench
of kelp and trench.

Are we going to laugh
on the road as if the whole
show was set out for our grand synthesis?
Abandoned trailers sunk in leaves and turf,
slow erosion, waves on the boil . . .
We belong to this —

not as discrete
observing presences but as born
participants in the action, sharing of course
'the seminal substance of the universe'
with hedgerow, flower and thorn,
rook, rabbit and rat.

These longer days
bursting with sunlit fruit
and some vague confidence inspire besides
skittish bacteria, fungi, viruses, gastropods
squirming in earth and dirt.
Dark energies,

resisting gravity,
fling farther the red-shifting gas
but the lone bittern and the red grouse,
crying 'Go back!', have got the measure of it.
Animal, vegetable, mineral watch
as we walk their patch;

and a bath in the woods,
its brown depths where once
a bubbling foam of soap and juniper.
Now tar-water of Cloyne, cow faces, clouds,
ice of the winter months
and nobody there.

Nobody there
for days and nights but our own
curious thoughts in a storm or before dawn.
Bird, beast and flower, whatever your names are,
like the wind blowing through
we belong here too.

Homage to Gaia

I ITS RADIANT ENERGIES

A world of dikes and bikes
   where yoghurt-weavers drive
on gin and margarine . . .
   This is how to live

in the post-petroleum age,
   gathering light-beams
to run the house with clean
   photoelectric frames

that trap the sun and focus
   its radiant energies;
their glow reflects the seasons,
   cloud cover, open skies.

Our micro-climate gives us
   gentle winters here.
Spring starts in January
   and lasts throughout the year

with its perennial flowers,
   so even an average annual
thousand kilowatt hours
   per photovoltaic panel

looks feasible in time.
   What you notice about
the panes is their composure,
   their heliotropic quiet

as star-gazing, rain-laced,
   light-drinking polysilicon

raises its many faces
   to worship the hot sun.

Great sun, dim or bright,
   eye in the changing sky,
send us warmth and light!
   We can never die

while you are roaring there
   in serial rebirth
far from our atmosphere.
   Remember life on Earth!

Since we destroyed the woods
    with crazy chainsaws, oiled
the sea, burned up the clouds,
    upset the natural world

to grow fat, if I may
    I want to apologize
for our mistakes and pay
    homage to seas and skies,

to field and stream; to you,
    great Gaia our first mother
with your confused retinue
    of birds, your weird weather.

You've done so much for us
    and what do we give back?
Suspension bridges, yes,
    and columns of black smoke.

Blowing hot and cold,
    you love us and hate us both;
we babble about the world
    while you sustain the earth.

You will prevail of course
    if in a different form;
we go from bad to worse
    just trying to keep warm.

3 WIND AND WAVE

Quixote would pick a fight
    with wind turbines, more
bad giants gesticulating
    from onshore and offshore —

not realizing that these
    and the far-sighted wave
fetching up from long
    seas with a final heave

transform the wild energies
    of chaos and old night
into a clean and infinite
    source of power and light.

Coleridge kept an Aeolian
    harp like a harmonica
lodged in an open window
    to catch the slightest flicker

of even the faintest breeze
    in even the calmest weather,
the Muse of music dozing
    upon her quiet zither —

for this is the true breath
    of life, the air that sings
in larynx and sea froth
    and ruffles the spread wings;

this is the wind that drives
    the dark waves below

to light our homely lives
   with an unearthly glow.

Blow, wind, and seize
   the slick rotors! Race,
tide, to the estuaries
   so we shine on in Space!

4 SAND AND STARS

The night life of the shore:
   rock music, flashing light.
Increasingly I prefer
   to get an early night;

yet here I am, listening
   again to a cold strand,
the vast sky glistening
   like blown dust or sand.

Ancient shingle races,
   clicking and sparkling, down
to wild watery chaos.
   As for the twinkly town,

roofed like a sea surface
   with moonlit tiles, the eye
measures its tiny houses
   against an enormous sky.

Gardens find their right
   higher and lower levels;
rockeries stagger out
   like underwater shelves.

High tide among the pines,
   cod caves in the boughs,
plaice flap in the ruins
   of sunken bungalows.

5 AT URSULA'S

A cold and stormy morning.
   I sit in Ursula's place
and fancy something spicy
   served with the usual grace

by one of her bright workforce
   who know us from before,
a nice girl from Tbilisi,
   Penang or Baltimore.

Some red basil linguine
   would surely hit the spot,
something light and shiny,
   mint-yoghurty and hot;

a frosty but delightful
   pistachio ice-cream
and some strong herbal
   infusion wreathed in steam.

Once a tomato sandwich
   and a pint of stout would do
but them days are over.
   I want to have a go

at some amusing fusion
   Thai and Italian both,
a dish of squid and pine-nuts
   simmered in lemon broth,

and catch the atmospherics,
   the happy lunchtime crowd,

as the cold hand gets warmer
  and conversation loud.

Boats strain at sea, alas,
  gales rattle the slates
while inside at Ursula's
  we bow to our warm plates.

6 LONDON RAIN

It raps at the skylights
   of Soho flats, a vast
vertical downpour long
   awaited, here at last

panicking car alarms,
   making the windows gleam
and rinsing hot roof tiles
   in clouds of rising steam.

It hoses the back doors
   of the very first highrise
car park in London
   where I've checked for days

on the speaking, anachronistic
   fate of a paint blister
scraped and flaking into
   a heap of dust and plaster.

Buses and taxis thrash
   under a thundery sky,
tracking down Regent St.
   'To shops in crowds' they fly

as if from an air-raid
   in the strange early dark.
Rain falls like space debris
   on Brick Lane, Hyde Park,

St Paul's and Primrose Hill,
   streams down as it used to do

for whole hours at a stretch
    on evenings long ago.

But this is a new rain
    the rainmakers have sent,
corporate and imported
    to swamp a continent.

Earthquake and tsunami!
    Wasteful and cackling, Thames
water still bubbles away
    as in more temperate times.

Euphoric as it crashes
    riotously from the tap,
it still flows and twinkles
    as if it will never stop —

even when a rainbow drips
    above Bayswater, the sky turns
to a glistening denim-blue
    and an evening star shines.

Think of this abundance
    when the bright splatter blows
eastwards, leaving the heavens
    a washed-out yellow-rose.

7 ODE TO BJÖRK

Dark bird of ice, dark swan
   of snow, your bright gamine
teardrop Inuit eyes
   peep from a magazine

as if to say 'Fuck off
   and get my new release;
you don't know *me*, I am
   the dark swan of ice

and secrecy, the seagull,
   the unringed plover, not
something to tame and stroke.'
   Ever since Spit & Snot,

'Aeroplane' and 'Anchor Song'
   your aim has been to knock
aside the expectations
   of corporate brainwash rock.

'Headphones' and 'Cover Me',
   I listen to your voice,
a lonely bird that pipes
   from quickly thawing ice,

a bad child acting out
   behind the electronics,
a mad flirt and shout
   beyond the audio mix.

No doubt you'd like to get
   an open car, a megaphone

and tell the world like Garbo
    'I want to be alone!'

Here in the confused stink
    of global warming what
you really want, I think,
    is not spit 'n' snot

but mystery and mystique,
    the hidden places where
the wild things are and no one
    can track you to your lair.

(Sea levels rising annually,
    glaciers sliding fast,
species extinct, the far north
    negotiable at last . . .)

Anyhow you're not playing
    to us, are you, but to the white
light and corrugated iron
    roofs of the Arctic night.

Up there where silence falls
    and there is no more land
your scared, scary voice calls
    to the great waste beyond.

8 DIRIGIBLES

We who used to drift
   superbly in mid-air,
each a giant airship
   before 'the last war',

shrink to a soft buzz
   above financial centres
surprising visitors,
   hackers and bean counters

in cloud-flown highrises.
   Cloud-slow, we snoop for hours
on open-plan offices
   and cloudy cocktail bars.

Amnesia and mystique
   have cast into oblivion
fiery failures like
   Italia, R101,

the whole brief catalogue
   of mad catastrophes;
and showy *Hindenburg*
   of course, the last of these.

A temporary setback.
   Our time will come again
with helium in the sack
   instead of hydrogen

while slow idealists
   gaze at refrozen ice,

reflourishing rain forests,
   the oceans back in place;

at sand and stars, blue skies,
   clear water, scattered light
as in the early days
   of nearly silent flight.

9 INDIAN GARDEN

Indigo night fronds like
    quills dipped in ink
share in the life cycle
    as quietly they drink

the close tropical heat.
    New coconuts take shape
in clusters out of reach,
    'patrimony of the ape'

said Durrell. A well-aimed
    machete stroke; you sip
nectar, and the brainy
    skull is its own cup.

It rots in sandy soil
    here at the ocean rim,
changing to coal and oil
    through geological time.

The spiritual substance
    we generate likewise
rejoins the ancient dance.
    It never wholly dies

but circulates at random
    somewhere in the ether
when body closes down;
    and so we live for ever.

Turtle Beach

Black laterite outcrops ranged along
the seaboard shield them from the most
alarming feature of this coast,
mud chaos of the rainy months —
but not from parties, thong and song,
when the new people dance the dance.

The crow and the high Brahminy kite
know about the amphibious chicks
due to emerge on hatching night
and flipper-scramble down the shore.
The toughs are up to their old tricks,
looking out for a chance to score;

but still the turtles once a year
head for nest-sites up the beach:
the human footprint doesn't scare
these creatures from their sanctuary.
Only night-sight cameras watch
the young in their wild dash to the sea.

Goa

Homage to Goa

The ceiling fans in the house go round and round
as if to whisk us off to a different sky.
I squirt Deet at a thin mosquito whine;
gods chuckle softly from a garden shrine,
fruit ripen in the gloaming without a sound.
Shiva, Parvati and Ganesh the elephant boy
promote the comical to the sublime; though, shown
a choice of deities, I defer like most
to violet Krishna in the heat and dust,
brother of Dionysus, expert in everything —
flute-player, hero and lecher, comedian, king.

I rock on a warm veranda as daylight goes.
The hippies too revered him in the old days
of hair and beads, torchlight and techno trance,
trailing from poppy field to lamasery
as irksome and imperious as Camões.
It's snowing in Kashmir, but here in Goa
we already have spring temperatures. Anandu
waters the earth and brushes up the sand.
Banana leaves and plantains in a daze
trade oxygen for tar; *tat tvam asi*.
Already a heavy mango strikes the ground.

A mozzie once myself, *I* buzzed and bit —
but only foot and elbow, ear and knee;
a cheeky monkey keen on human thought,
with a reach greater than my grasp, I'd dance
wildly at times, conscious of ignorance,
or chew on my own morose inadequacy.
Still, I behaved, and so the next time out
I got to sit to a half-mad sadhu
at Brahmin school. 'The body is a shadow,'
said he, 'it tells you in the Upanishads';
but spirit knows no slapstick or romance.

Clouds dream the people and we spread like plants,
waves smash on beaches for no obvious purpose
except to deliver the down-to-earth palingenesis
of multitudinous life particles. A porpoise
revolves on the sky as if in outer space
where we started out so many aeons ago.
Goa fact file: infant mortality low,
average life expectancy seventy-five,
functional literacy sixty-nine percent;
the porcupine and flying fox survive,
also the sloth bear and shy Chital doe.

'The streaming meteor, is it dead or alive,
a deliberate thing or merely gas and stone?
Some believe in a life after this one
while others say we're only nut and leaf.
An ageing man repents his wicked ways:
we began so innocently, and may again'
— Abu al-Ma'ari, tenth century, Syrian.
Given a choice between paradise and this life
I'd choose this life with its calamities,
the shining sari, the collapsing wave,
the jeep asleep beneath the coconut trees;

skyflower, flame-of-the-forest among the palms,
ripe mangoes dropping from the many limbs,
the radio twang of a high-pitched sitar,
'Kareena Kapoor in Hot New Avatar'!
A gecko snaps a spider from a window.
Given a choice of worlds, here or beyond,
I'd pick this one not once but many times
whether as mozzie, monkey or pure mind.
The road to enlightenment runs past the house
with its auto-rickshaws and its dreamy cows
but the fans, like the galaxies, go round and round.

Many of these poems were published first by The Gallery Press in limited editions: *Art Notes,* with drawings by Vivienne Roche (2006), *Somewhere the Wave*, with drawings and watercolours by Bernadette Kiely (2007) and *Homage to Gaia*, with drawings by Hammond Journeaux (2008).